Blom

A Story of Fashion Designer
Elsa Schiaparelli

Words by

KYO MACLEAR

Pictures by

JULIE MORSTAD

HARPER
An Imprint of HarperCollinsPublishers

Every story starts somewhere.

My story begins on September 10, 1890, in a beautiful palazzo in the center of Roma. That's in Italy.

Imagine a quiet room. Imagine a newborn baby looking up to see her pappa frowning, her mamma frowning.

Disappointed that I am not a boy, they have no
name for me! They borrow a name from a nurse. Elsa.

They say it like this: El-za.

IT'S ALL WRONG FOR ME!

Now I am frowning.

One day, I snuggle deep in my carriage. I am alone. Except for the flowers.

All around, they are waving and smiling: HELLO!

All I see is PINK.

Bright, bold, shocking pink!

The color swirls inside me.

My home is dark and gray, but it doesn't matter because all around Roma there is COLOR.

And JOY.

My sister, Beatrice, is Mamma's favorite.
She is ten years older.
"Bella," Mamma says.

And me?

"Brutta."

I hate to have my picture taken.

Visiting Roma's flower market one morning,
I lose myself in a dazzling stream of colors,
shapes, and smells.

Ah! Sweet *canella*, fragrant *melone*, a bouquet
of *fiori*.

Bold beauty. Quiet beauty.
Hidden beauty.

By the age of seven, I wonder:

What makes something beautiful?

Will I ever be as pretty as a peony,
as confident as a daisy?

A seed seller pins a flower to my dress.
It is strange but wonderful.

He has given me AN IDEA.

I run home to see the family gardener.
The next day I plant flower seeds in my
ears, mouth, and nose.

"To have a face covered
        with flowers like
a heavenly garden would indeed
        be a wonderful thing!"

I sit and wait.
Wait to bloom.
Wait to bloom.

By nightfall, I am breathless and sick.
It takes two doctors to remove the
seeds. My plan flops, but a different
kind of seed is planted . . .

...a seed of wild imagination.

That summer, my family travels to Milano to visit Uncle Giovanni.

Uno, due, tre... my sister counts the seven moles on my left cheek.

Giovanni is a famous astronomer. A dreamer. We spend hours together peering through his telescope at the stars.

"There are people on Mars just like us," he says.
"They are probably making polenta right now."

"Come on, mia cara," he says.
"Voliamo. Let's fly."

I still feel brutta, but my
uncle lifts me up, up, up.
He tells me my moles are as
beautiful as the Big Dipper.

Back at home, with an umbrella in my hand,
I leap out a third-floor window. I imagine
soaring like da Vinci's flying machine, before
landing in the gardener's manure pile.

Ideas are everywhere I look:
among the books in my father's
library, among the trunks of
dresses and objects belonging to
my mother in the attic.

I am an explorer, a circus performer, and even the night sky. Dress up. Pretend. Make believe. The world feels brighter.

I am growing into an artist.

But to be an artist, it takes money! At age twenty-two, I take a job in England as a nanny. On a brief stop in Paris, a friend invites me to a ball.

With a few francs, I go to a department store and PRESTO! I design my first dress. It is held together with a few pins. No time to sew!

I am a queen floating and sailing across the dance floor. Until the pins give way . . .

The dress is a disaster, but my passion for dressmaking is sparked.

Moving from city to city, Paris, London, and finally New York, seven years hurtle by. Nothing is permanent, but one thing remains constant: I keep making clothes. For myself, for my friends, for my new husband (we are together only briefly), for my darling baby daughter, Gogo.

I draw my ideas on paper, making up my own rules along the way. It is 1921, and now I call myself "Schiap."

Can I do what I love and still provide for Gogo?

To be an artist is to dream big and risk failure.

Gogo is two in 1922 when I decide to return to Paris. I am broke, nervous, excited, and ready to burst. But it's time to show the world my sketches.

I start each morning filled with hope, braving rejection, stumbling home on tired legs. I want to give up but I don't. I will not be beaten.

In my heart, Uncle Giovanni is cheering me on.

Our cold-water apartment is dreary,
but friendship lifts me. Through my pal
Gaby Picabia, I fall in with a pack of artists.

We must be
outrageous!
-Salvador Dali

We are
artists,
not
dressmakers!
-Paul Poiret

We share our crazy dreams.

One day, I am introduced to
Mike, a knitting *maestra*.

"If I make a design, will you try
to knit it?" I ask.

"We will try," she says.

We try. And try. I am more determined than ever.

Until finally . . .

SENSAZIONALE!

My big breakthrough!
Trompe l'oeil. We have created
the illusion of a bowknot.

Women go wild for the
modern design.

At the late-blooming age of thirty-seven, I open my first shop.

It is soon the beating heart of Paris.

The new world is buzzing. Women don't want to just sit around looking pretty. They want to DREAM and DO bold things.

My unique clothes invite women to express their imaginations fully.

A thread of doubt remains inside me. I know Mamma, Pappa, and Beatrice in Roma will never approve of the path I have taken.

But I no longer feel *brutta*. For the first time, I see the beauty
of my art reflected in the world.

Boundless, unstoppable. My fingers itch to combine the strangest materials. WHY NOT lace with leather, wool with cellophane, tree bark and velvet? A face of flowers may be impossible, but WHY NOT a shoe on my head, a coat with many drawers, a lobster dress?

I say NO to the expected.

I say YES to my childhood dreams and the colors that once fed me: scarlet, mauve, periwinkle, green . . .

. . . and PINK!

My friend the chemist Jean Clément helps me mix a
new color for my next collection of dresses and hats.

Jean adds more red. "Not quite," I say.

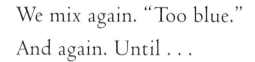

We mix again. "Too blue."
And again. Until . . .

PERFECTION!

"The color flashed
in front of my eyes.
Bright, impossible, impudent,
becoming, life-giving,
like all the light and the birds and
the fish in the world put together."

Wild and explosive! I call it SHOCKING PINK.
The fashion world spins with panic and delight.

Not everything I make is a success,
but through my work a wondrous thing happens.

I free myself from Mamma's harsh words
and Pappa's judgment.

I free myself to be daring, different, and whole.

I plant a new seed of beauty.

Beauty itself blooms to reveal the irregular, the
imperfect, the smart, tough, goofy, surreal, and wild.

The women I inspire, and the women who inspire
me, and the girl I was, who once felt so ugly that she
planted seeds on her face . . .

All of us, together: We BLOOM and BLOOM.

Elsa Schiaparelli

(pronounced "SKYAP-a-relli")

1890–1973

A Note from the Author and the Illustrator

Born in Rome to a strict aristocratic family, Elsa Schiaparelli grew up to become one of the world's most original and influential fashion designers. Her madly inventive clothes and singular sense of style radically changed the look of fashion in the 1920s and 1930s, and her clothes were worn and celebrated by some of history's most adventurous and creative women, including Amelia Earhart, Greta Garbo, and Marlene Dietrich.

Rejecting the idea that women's fashion should be overly feminine and plain, Schiaparelli embraced the bold and playful. She collaborated with the surrealists and leading avant-garde artists to create colorful and sometimes outrageous outfits. In Schiaparelli's eyes, nothing was too common or strange to be turned into an object of unusual and intriguing beauty. She saw no lines between art and fashion, the ordinary and the fantastical. Having never learned to sew, she worked with talented cutters, seamstresses, and embroiderers to bring her sketches and flamboyant dreams to life.

It is difficult to express everything she was and did in such a short book, so we thought we would end with a brief catalog of her contributions.

She invented and/or redefined: the jumpsuit, the wraparound dress, see-through raincoats, paper clothes, fun fur, folding eyeglasses, and colored tights.

She used: exposed zippers, wacky buttons, crumpled fabric, pink, pink, pink . . . and "ice blue" (another color she famously introduced).

Schiaparelli's motto was "Dare to be different," and she was. She showed the world what it meant to be led by nerve and imagination, to defy your critics and doubts. She modeled a truly artful and collaborative life and to this day inspires artists across disciplines (ourselves included!). Look around and you'll see her enduring influence in design houses and on runways around the world.

She made: a cocktail hat in the shape of a lamb chop, a skeleton dress with a padded rib cage, and a suit with "bureau drawer" pockets.

She collaborated with: Salvador Dalí, Jean Cocteau, Man Ray, Leonor Fini, Alberto Giacometti, Raoul Dufy, Cecil Beaton, and other fantastically imaginative artists of her day.

She was the first fashion designer to: open a "ready-to-wear" boutique, use music and circus performers in a fashion show, introduce men's suits in a women's collection, and offer high wages and benefits to her employees.

*For my mom
(with garlands for Julie, Jill, Tara, Amy, Erin, and Jackie)
—K.M.*

*To the memory of my grandmother, Marion,
and her innate sense of color and style
—J.M.*

ENDNOTES

"To have a face covered with flowers": Elsa Schiaparelli, *Shocking Life: The Autobiography of Elsa Schiaparelli* (London: J. M. Dent & Sons, 1954), 17.

"The color flashed in front of my eyes": Schiaparelli, *Shocking Life*, 114.

Artist dialogue on pages 22–23 inspired by the following:

Salvador Dalí: *"The one thing the world will never have enough of is the outrageous."* Salvador Dalí, *Diary of a Genius* (Garden City, NY: Doubleday, 1965), entry for August 30, 1953.

Alberto Giacometti: *"The more you fail, the more you succeed."* *A Man Among Men: Alberto Giacometti.* Directed by Jean-Marie Drot, 1963.

Meret Oppenheim: *"Freedom is not given to you—you have to take it."* Belinda Grace Gardner, *Meret Oppenheim: From Breakfast in Fur and Back Again*, edited by Thomas Levy (Bielefeld, Germany: Kerber Verlag, 2003), 7.

Pablo Picasso: *"All children are artists. The problem is how to remain an artist once he grows up."* www.pablopicasso.org/quotes.jsp.

Paul Poiret: *"I am an artist, not a dressmaker."* "Paul Poiret Here to Tell of His Art," *New York Times*, September 21, 1913, 11.

SOURCES AND FURTHER READING

Blum, Dilys E. *Shocking! The Art and Fashion of Elsa Schiaparelli*. New Haven: Yale University Press, 2003.

Martin, Richard. *Fashion and Surrealism*. New York: Rizzoli, 1990.

Rubin, Susan Goldman. *Hot Pink: The Life and Fashions of Elsa Schiaparelli*. New York: Harry N. Abrams, 2015.

Schiaparelli, Elsa. *Shocking Life: The Autobiography of Elsa Schiaparelli*. London: J. M. Dent & Sons, 1954.

Secrest, Meryle. *Elsa Schiaparelli: A Biography*. New York: Alfred A. Knopf, 2014.

Volk, Patricia. *Shocked: My Mother, Schiaparelli, and Me*. New York: Alfred A. Knopf, 2013.

Bloom: A Story of Fashion Designer Elsa Schiaparelli
Text copyright © 2018 by Kyo Maclear
Illustrations copyright © 2018 by Julie Morstad
All rights reserved. Manufactured in China.
No part of this book may be used or reproduced in any manner whatsoever without written permission except in the case of brief quotations embodied in critical articles and reviews. For information address HarperCollins Children's Books, a division of HarperCollins Publishers, 195 Broadway, New York, NY 10007.
www.harpercollinschildrens.com

Library of Congress Control Number: 2017934827
ISBN 978-0-06-244761-6

The artist used liquid watercolor, gouache, and pencil crayons to create the illustrations for this book.
Typography by Erin Fitzsimmons and Julie Morstad
18 19 20 21 22 SCP 10 9 8 7 6 5 4 3 2 1

❖

First Edition